First World War
and Army of Occupation
War Diary
France, Belgium and Germany

14 DIVISION
42 Infantry Brigade
Duke of Edinburgh's (Wiltshire Regiment)
6th Battalion
1 June 1918 - 9 June 1919

WO95/1902/2

The Naval & Military Press Ltd
www.nmarchive.com
Published in association with The National Archives

Published by

The Naval & Military Press Ltd

Unit 10 Ridgewood Industrial Park,

Uckfield, East Sussex,

TN22 5QE England

Tel: +44 (0) 1825 749494

www.naval-military-press.com

www.nmarchive.com

This diary has been reprinted in facsimile from the original. Any imperfections are inevitably reproduced and the quality may fall short of modern type and cartographic standards.

© Crown Copyright
Images reproduced by permission of The National Archives, London, England, 2015.

Contents

Document type	Place/Title	Date From	Date To
Heading	14th Division 42nd Infy Bde 6th Bn Wilts Regt Jun 1918-Jun 1919 From 19 Div 58 Bde		
Heading	War Diary Of 6th Wilts Regt. From 1-6-18 To 30-6-18 Volume No 36		
War Diary	Melleville Dieppe Sheet	01/06/1918	15/06/1918
War Diary	Gamaches Dieppe Sheet	16/06/1918	16/06/1918
War Diary	Boulogne	16/06/1918	16/06/1918
War Diary	Brookwood	17/06/1918	30/06/1918
Heading	War Diary Of 6th Wilts Regt. From 1-7-18 to 31-7-18 volume No. 37		
War Diary	Brookwood	01/07/1918	02/07/1918
War Diary	Folkestone	03/07/1918	03/07/1918
War Diary	Calais 13	04/07/1918	12/07/1918
War Diary	Hazebrouck 5A.	13/07/1918	15/07/1918
War Diary	Sheet No 27	16/07/1918	31/07/1918
Heading	6th Wiltshire Regiment. War Diary. From. 1.8.18 to 31.8.18. Volume No. 38.		
War Diary		01/08/1918	31/08/1918
Heading	War Diary Of 6th Wilts Regt. From 1-9-18 to 30-9-18 Volume No 39		
War Diary		01/09/1918	30/09/1918
Miscellaneous	Narrative of Operations, 6th Battn, Wiltshire Regt. at St. Eloi 29.8.18	30/09/1918	30/09/1918
Heading	War Diary 6th Batt Wiltshire Regt. Oct 1st-31st 1918 Volume 40		
War Diary		01/10/1918	31/10/1918
Heading	6th Batt Wiltshire Regt. War Diary 1st-30th November 1918 Volume 40		
War Diary	Field	01/11/1918	30/11/1918
Heading	War Diary 6th Battn Wiltshire Regiment. From December 1st To December 31st 1918 Volume 36 Vol 44		
War Diary		01/12/1918	31/12/1918
Heading	War Diary 6th Bn Wiltshire Regt Jan 1st 1919 To Jany 31st 1919 Volume 41 Vol 45		
War Diary		01/01/1919	31/01/1919
Heading	6th Battalion Wiltshire Regt War Diary 1st-28th February 1918 Vol 42 Vol 46		
War Diary	Wattrelos	01/02/1919	31/03/1919
War Diary	Wattrelos France	01/04/1919	30/04/1919
Heading	War Diary 6th Bn Wiltshire Regt From May 1st 1919 To May 31st 1919 Volume 36		
War Diary	Wattrelos France	01/05/1919	17/05/1919
War Diary	Wattrelos	18/05/1919	31/05/1919
Heading	War Diary 6th Battn Wiltshire Regt From 1-6-19 To 9-6-19 Volume 36		
War Diary	Wattrelos	01/06/1919	09/06/1919

14TH DIVISION
42ND INFY BDE

6TH BN WILTS REGT
JUN 1918-JUN 1919

CONFIDENTIAL

WAR DIARY

OF

6th Wilts Regt

FROM 1-6-18 TO 30-6-18

VOLUME NO. 36

Army Form C. 2118.

WAR DIARY
or
INTELLIGENCE SUMMARY.
(Erase heading not required.)

Instructions regarding War Diaries and Intelligence Summaries are contained in F.S. Regs., Part II. and the Staff Manual respectively. Title pages will be prepared in manuscript.

Place	Date	Hour	Summary of Events and Information	Remarks and references to Appendices
MELLEVILLE.	1st		Training	App.
	2nd		Sunday Church Parade	App.
DIEPPE	3rd		Training	App.
SHEET 4	4th		Training	App.
	5th		Training	App.
	6th		2/159th Infantry Regt left MELLEVILLE. Guards sent out to LE MESNIL REAUME and CUVERVILLE to Guard Stores	App.
	7th		Training & Relaying of Billets vacated by 3/159 Inf Regt	App.
	8th		Training & Relaying of Billets vacated by 2/159 Inf Regt	App.
	9th		Sunday Church Parade	App.
	10th		Advance Billeting Party of 3/125 Inf Regt arrived. Arrangements for Billeting completed	App.
	11th		3/125 Inf Regt arrived in Billets at 4 pm	App.
	12th		Troops and Horses of 3/125 Inf Regt taken over by 3 P.C. Reform.	App.
	13th		Training for duty and demand Commence	App.
	14th		Training Orders received for escorts to be forwarded to Infanta on 15th inst	App.
	15th		Reporting to same, Orders received that Bn Hors. Drawn and Forwards to Infanta. Left Billets at MELLEVILLE 12 n.	App.

WAR DIARY
or
INTELLIGENCE SUMMARY.

(Erase heading not required.)

Army Form C. 2118.

Place	Date	Hour	Summary of Events and Information	Remarks and references to Appendices
EAMACHES DIEPPE SHEET	16th	6.30 pm	and marched to EAMACHES Station where the Battalion (strength 9 Offrs + 441 O/Ranks) entrained for BOULOGNE at 12 m.n.	15/16th
BOULOGNE	17th		Marching to BOULOGNE. Arrived at OSTROOVE CAMP BOULOGNE at 6.30 p.m. Cpl B. Ayo Lochen + Lt Bathit joined O.C.M. + Stettings Lt. Dopt. and 2nd Lieut J Gillmore joined for duty.	c.f.
			Entrained BOULOGNE 11 am arriving at FOLKESTONE 2 p.m.	
BROOKWOOD			Entrained at FOLKESTONE 4.30 p.m. + arrived at BROOKWOOD Station 8.30 p.m. + marched to BULLSWATER Camp	c.f.
	18th		Cleaning up etc. 42 O/Ranks join for duty.	c.f.
	19th		33 Officers + 620 O/Ranks join from 9th London to Battalion moved at 2 p.m. to COWSHOTT CAMP 78, Bisley.	c.f.
	20th		Organisation of Battalion orders received that Battalion will be known as 6th (Reserve) Yeomanry Sussex Regt.	c.f.
	21st		Organisation of Battalion. 191 O/Ranks join for duty.	c.f.
	22nd		Organisation + Refitting of Battalion. 30 O/Ranks join for duty.	c.f.
	23rd		Organisation + Refitting of Battalion. 21 O/Ranks join for duty.	c.f.
	24th		Organisation + Refitting of Battalion. 2 O/Ranks join for duty	c.f.

WAR DIARY
or
INTELLIGENCE SUMMARY.
(Erase heading not required.)

Army Form C. 2118.

Place	Date	Hour	Summary of Events and Information	Remarks and references to Appendices
BROOKWOOD	25th		Wire received that Drums is to embark for Havana on 29th inst.	n/a
	26th		Organization & training. Orders received that Drum must embark later.	n/a
	27th		Organization & training. 70 o/Ranks joined for duty.	n/a
	28th		Organization & training. 8 o/Ranks joined for duty.	n/a
	29th		Organization & training. Orders received for Drums to entrain for Havre from Brookwood on Jan. 1 o/Ranks for duty.	n/a
	30th		Organization & training. 435 Wight men detached to 3rd R Innis. Regt. Armoury.	n/a

J. F. Hayden Lieut. Col.
O. C. 6/ R. Ir. Regt
31-7-17

CONFIDENTIAL

WAR DIARY

OF

6TH WILTS. REGT.

FROM 1=7=18 TO 31=7=18

VOLUME NO. 37.

Army Form C. 2118.

WAR DIARY
or
INTELLIGENCE SUMMARY.
(Erase heading not required.)

Instructions regarding War Diaries and Intelligence Summaries are contained in F. S. Regs., Part II. and the Staff Manual respectively. Title pages will be prepared in manuscript.

Place	Date	Hour	Summary of Events and Information	Remarks and references to Appendices
BROOKWOOD	1st		Regt Transport left for overseas. Strength 2 Officers + 51 O/Ranks.	R777
			Training & re-organizing of Battn.	R777
"	2nd		Preparing for overseas.	R777
FOLKESTONE	3rd		Left Lowshott Camp entraining at Aporshoot & detraining at Morncliffe and marched to Rest Camp arriving there, "A" + "B" Coys. at 2 a.m. "C", "D" + HdQrs 3.30 a.m. Strength 36 Officers, 541 O/Ranks.	R777
CALAIS. 13.	4th		Embarked Folkestone 9 a.m., & disembarked Boulogne 11.45 a.m. marched to Ostrove Camp.	R777
	5th		Left Ostrove Camp 10 a.m. & marched to Capelle.	R777
	6th		Training & re-organization of Coys.	R777
	7th		Training & re-organization of Coys.	R777
	8th		Training & re-organization of Coys.	R777
	9th		Training & re-organization of Coys.	R777
	10th		Training & re-organization of Coys.	R777
	11th		Left LA CAPELLE 9 a.m. & marched to BOURSIN. Warning Order received that Battn. will proceed to WINNEZEELE tied at a later date.	R777
	12th		Left BOURSIN 9 a.m. & marched to LICQUES.	R777

WAR DIARY
or
INTELLIGENCE SUMMARY.
(Erase heading not required.)

Army Form C. 2118.

Place	Date	Hour	Summary of Events and Information	Remarks and references to Appendices
HAZEBROUCK 5A.	13th		Left LICQUES 9 a.m. & marched to NORDAUSQUES. Order received to proceed to WINNEZEELE before line on 16th	0277
	14th		Left NORDAUSQUES 9 a.m. & march to SERQUES. Battn. attached to 101st Inf. Bde.	0277
	15th		SERQUES. Cleaning up.	0277
SHEET No.27	16th		Battn. entrained at 9 a.m. & proceeded to camp at 7.19.d. I.O. near SYLVESTRE CAPPEL transport proceeded by road. Billeting at NOODEPEENE night of 16th.	0277
	17th		Cleaning up. Reconnoitring & Battn. Practice at 8.30 p.m. moving up to Positions of Defence. WINNEZEELE line.	0277
	18th		280 O/Ranks on Working Parties with R.E. Remainder of Battn. training.	0277
	19th		280 O/Ranks on Working Parties with R.E. Remainder of Battn. training. 2nd Lieut. J.A.DAWE joined for duty.	0277
	20th		280 O/Ranks on Working Parties with R.E. Remainder of Battn. training. 268 O/Ranks joined from Garrison Base Depot.	0277
	21st		Church Parade. Inspection of Draft.	0277
	22nd		310 O/Ranks on Working Parties. training of Draft. 2nd Lieut. A.R.E. SMITH and 9 O/Ranks joined from England.	0277
	23rd		510 O/Ranks on Working Parties with R.E. Remainder of Battn. training. Lewis Gun training.	0277
	24th		490 O/Ranks on Working Parties with R.E. Remainder of Battalion training.	0277

Army Form C. 2118.

WAR DIARY
or
INTELLIGENCE SUMMARY.
(Erase heading not required.)

Instructions regarding War Diaries and Intelligence Summaries are contained in F. S. Regs., Part II. and the Staff Manual respectively. Title pages will be prepared in manuscript.

Place	Date	Hour	Summary of Events and Information	Remarks and references to Appendices
	25th		380 O/Ranks on Working Parties with R.E. Bathing & training.	R.77
	26th		495 O/Ranks on Working Parties with R.E. Remainder of Battn. training.	R.77
	27th		395 O/Ranks on Working Parties with R.E. Training & Bathing. Orders received re relief by O.Y.L.H. on 31st July	R.77
	28th		Sunday. Church Parade. L.O. inspection of Camp. 2nd Lieut. D.J. EVANS rejoined, & 1 O/Rank.	R.77
	29th		510 O/Ranks on Working Parties with R.E. Remainder of Battn. training.	R.77
	30th		485 O/Ranks on Working Parties with R.E. Remainder of Battn. training. Cleaning up & preparing for move.	R.77
	31st		Battn. moved at 8.30 a.m. & presumably marched route to NOORDPEENE. Battn. relieved in Forward Area by 14th R. + S.H.	R.77

J.F.E. Hodgson Lieut-Col
O.C. 6/11th R.W.F.
31-7-18

CONFIDENTIAL.

6th Wiltshire Regiment.

War Diary.

from.

1.8.18 to 31.8.18.

Volume No 38.

Army Form C. 2118.

WAR DIARY
or
INTELLIGENCE SUMMARY.
(Erase heading not required.)

Instructions regarding War Diaries and Intelligence Summaries are contained in F. S. Regs., Part II. and the Staff Manual respectively. Title pages will be prepared in manuscript.

Place	Date	Hour	Summary of Events and Information	Remarks and references to Appendices
	1st.		Battalion moved by March Route to SERQUES. Mens packs carried on Lorries Route via NOORDPEENE.	
	2nd.		Battalion moved by March Route to NORDAUSQUES.	
	3rd.		Bathing. Kit Inspection. 2nd.Lieut.I.Collins and 5 O.Rs. joined from U.K.	
	4th.		Church Parade. 2nd.Lieut.L.W.Poole joined from Base.	
	5th.		Divisional Horse Show at EMERLEQUES. Battalion placed 3rd in general aggregate for Infantry Battalions.	
	6th.		Training under Company arrangements. Specialists under Specialist Officers.	
	7th.		Training under Company arrangements. Specialists under Specialist Officers.	
	8th.		Training under Company arrangements. Specialists under Specialist Officers. Attack Scheme carried out by "A" Coy. successfully. G.O.C. 2nd. Army present.	
	9th.		Battalion training under Company arrangements. Capt. Mather proceeded to II Corps Reception Camp for duty.	
	10th.		Training. Orders received to detail 1 Officer and 20 O.Rs. to represent the Battalion at Inspection of Division by H.M.The King.	
	11th.		Inspection by H.M.The King of 14th Division. Lieut.E.H.Acason and 20 O.Rs. represent the Battalion. Church Parade.	
	12th.		Battalion Training under Company arrangements.	
	13th.		Battalion Training under Company Arrangements. Demonstration at III Corps Cyclist H.Qs. of Loading Transport. 4 Officers, 4 C.S.M. attended.	
	14th.		Training under Company arrangements.	

Army Form C. 2118.

WAR DIARY
or
INTELLIGENCE SUMMARY.
(Erase heading not required)

Instructions regarding War Diaries and Intelligence Summaries are contained in F.S. Regs., Part II and the Staff Manual respectively. Title pages will be prepared in manuscript.

Place	Date	Hour	Summary of Events and Information	Remarks and references to Appendices
	15th.		Training under Company arrangements. Bombing accident on range owing to premature ignition. 2 Casualties. Lecture by VII Corps representative on Counter Battery Work at ZOUAFQUES.	
	16th.		Battalion and Specialist Training. Inspection of Transport by G.O.C. Division. 2nd.Lieut.S.Porter joined from Base.	
	17th.		Battalion and Specialist Training. 2nd.Lieut.Paisley proceeded to report to War Office for Indian Army.	
	18th.		Church Parade. Lieut.&Qr.Mr.G.F.E.Rapson proceeded on leave to U.K.. Major C.Wallace takes over Command.	
	19th.		Company and Specialist Training.	
	20th.		Company and Specialist Training.	
	21st.		Battalion Training.	
	22nd.		Battalion Training under Company arrangements. Transport proceeded to PROVEN AREA by March Route.	
	23rd.		Battalion marched to NORKERQUE at 4 a.m. and entrained for PROVEN AREA. Reached Camp near ST. JAN TER BIEZEN 2 p.m.	
	24th.		Baths. Medical Officer's Inspection. 2nd.Lieut.H.M.Cornish joined from Base.	
	25th.		Church Parade. "A" Coy. proceeded to ST. OMER-CASSEL AREA on detached duty, Bridge Guarding etc.	

WAR DIARY
or
INTELLIGENCE SUMMARY.

(Erase heading not required.)

Army Form C. 2118.

Place	Date	Hour	Summary of Events and Information	Remarks and references to Appendices
	26th.		Working Parties under R.Es. 380 O.Rs. Lewis Gunners training of Nos. 1. and 2. of Teams.	
	27th.		Working Parties under R.Es. Trench construction near ST. JAN TER BIEZEN. Loading party to C.R.E. COUTHOVE CHATEAU	
	28th.		Company Training.	
	29th.		Battalion (less "A" Coy) entrain for BRAKE CAMP, POPERINGHE AREA at 6 p.m. arriving 7.30 p.m. Transport by road.	
	30th.		Reconnoitring Forward Area and Training.	
	31st.		Reconnoitring Forward Area and Training. 2nd.Lieut.B.E.Partridge and 2nd.Lieut.H.Plumbley join for duty.	

CONFIDENTIAL

WAR DIARY

OF

6th WILTS REGT

FROM 1-9-18 TO 30-9-18

VOLUME NO

39

Army Form C. 2118.

WAR DIARY
or
INTELLIGENCE SUMMARY.
(Erase heading not required.)

Instructions regarding War Diaries and Intelligence Summaries are contained in F. S. Regs., Part II. and the Staff Manual respectively. Title pages will be prepared in manuscript.

Place	Date	Hour	Summary of Events and Information	Remarks and references to Appendices
	Apr. 1		Battalion in Reserve at BRAKE CAMP. 1 O.R. joined from D.I.B.D. Church Parade. Inspection of Billets by C.O.	9177
	2		Working Party 100 O.Rs. working on trenches near VLAMERTINGHE. Platoon training for remainder of Battn.	9177
	3		Platoon training. Working Parties of 150 O.Rs. at VLAMERTINGHE Chateau. " 16 O.Rs. at Bvl. Bomb Stores.	9177
	4		Platoon training. Working Parties of 150 O.Rs. at VLAMERTINGHE Chateau. " 16 O.Rs. at Bvl. Bomb Stores.	9177
			Orders received that Battn. will relieve 29th D.L.I. YPRES Section on 5.9.18. F.G.C.M. on Pte. HAYWOOD held in Lines. Advance Party 5 Officers 31 O.Rs. proceed to 11. a.o.8 at 8 p.m. to take over from 29th D.L.I in YPRES Sector.	
	5		Battn. less Transport, 'A' Coy & Qr. Mr. details entrained at TRIANGLE at 8.45 p.m. detrained GOODERICH and took over Reserve Lines. Battn. H.Qrs. at RAMPARTS YPRES. 1.8.a.1.7. Relief Complete 12 midnight.	9177
	6		Battn. in Reserve. Working Party of 6 Platoons at 8.45 p.m. Lieut. Col. Repson returned from leave & took over Command of 42nd Inf. Bde.	9177
	7		'A' Coy. rejoined Battn. from detached duty & took over reserve Coy. trenches in I.d.o.8.	9177
	8		Working Parties of 9 Platoons in YPRES area. Coy. Commanders reconnoitre Right Sub. Front.	9177

WAR DIARY or INTELLIGENCE SUMMARY

Army Form C. 2118.

Place	Date	Hour	Summary of Events and Information	Remarks and references to Appendices
	9		Working Party of 9 Platoons. 1 O.R. wounded remained at duty.	APP.
	10		Working Party of 9 Platoons. 2nd Lieut. B.J. Emerson wounded on duty.	APP.
	11		Working Party of 9 Platoons.	APP.
	12		Working Parties of 9 Platoons. Officers reconnoitre Front line & Right front line gas projectors on HALFWAY House. I.14.e.4.5. Also 21 N.W. 1/20,000. DORMY House. I.23.a.5.4. Map 28 N.W. 1/10000	APP.
	13		Battn. relieved by 33rd London Regt. & Rifle Bde. Party complete 12 midnight. 1 O.R. wounded.	APP.
	14		Battn. entrained 1 a.m. GOODERICH Station, detrained TRIANGLE 3.30 a.m. marched to DIRTY BUCKET CAMP arriving 4 a.m. Working Party of 2/2 Platoon found. Cleaning up & inspections. Lieut. C.E. Morgan returned on leave. Orders received for Battn. will move to WINNEZEELE Area.	APP.
	15		Battn. entrained TRIANGLE 11 a.m. detrained STEENVOORDE Junction 2.30 p.m. Transport proceeding by road. Battn. H.Q. at K.25.c.3.2. About 24 V/30,000. Companies billets in forward area.	APP.
	16		Training under Company arrangements.	APP.
	17		Training under Company arrangements.	APP.
	18		Training under Company arrangement. Battn. bathing at STEENVOORDE. "C" Coy inspected by G.O.C. 11 Corps. Orders received that Battn. would relieve 15th Bn. Sherwood Foresters in the CANAL Sector on 19.9.18. Advance party of 1 Officer & 3 O.R. proceeded to take over.	APP.

WAR DIARY
INTELLIGENCE SUMMARY

Army Form C. 2118.

Place	Date	Hour	Summary of Events and Information	Remarks and references to Appendices
	19		Batt. all Officers and OR entrained STEENVOORDE Junction detraining at YALE Junction 10.30 p.m. & marched to line Batt. H.Qrs. at N.24.c.5.3. 'A' Coy. left front C near SPOIL BANK I.33.a. to I.33.c. 'B' Coy. right front I.32.a. to I.31.d. 'B' left at I.25.c.t.d. 'D' Coy. reserve near Batt. H.Q. SURPLUS Personnel. 5 Officers 108 OR proceeded to 41st Div. Reception Camp PEESLE. Transport by road to G.52.a. Sheet 28 N.M. 1/40.000.	App.
	20		Batt. in line. Quiet day. Some shelling. 'A' Coy. 2 Casualties. 'C' Coy. 1 Casualty.	App.
	21		Relieved by 10th H.L.I. relief complete 2.30 a.m. Embussed at DICKEBUSH & proceeded to billets OUDERZEELE area, arriving 5.30 a.m. Transport & Surplus Personnel remaining at their camps.	App.
	22		Resting & cleaning up.	App.
	23		Training under Company arrangements. Orders received that Battn. will relieve 16th Manchester Regt. in line on night 25/26 Sept.	App.
	24		Training under Company arrangements. Orders received that the 42nd Bde. will attack German position at GT. ELOI on 7 day with two Battalions in the line. 6th H.L.I. on L. A.& S.H. on R. Assembly to be held FRENCH TRENCH.	App.
	25		Orders received for move to Front line DICKEBUSH sector on 26.9.18. Battalion move to new billets in STEENVOORDE Area by road leaving at 4.30 p.m. Battalion in billets by 8.30 p.m.	App.

Army Form C. 2118.

WAR DIARY
or
INTELLIGENCE SUMMARY.
(Erase heading not required.)

Place	Date	Hour	Summary of Events and Information	Remarks and references to Appendices
	26		Battalion entrained at STEENVOORDE Junction at 5.40pm and detrained YALE Junction 9.30pm. "A" & "C" Coys. taking over Monteire Dundee from 16th Manchesters at OLD FRENCH TRENCH, VOORMAZEELE. B. Coy in support at H.30.d.33. "D" Coy in reserve at H.24.a.29. Battalion Headquarters at A. BUND, DICKEBUSH.	RPT.
	27		Watches synchronised at 3pm and 10pm. Orders received at 5.30am that Zero hour will be 5.50am on 28th September. Support & Reserve Coys. moved up to assembly positions OLD FRENCH TRENCH. D. Coy in reserve in VOORMAZEELE Switch.	RPT.
	28		Narrative attached	RPT.
	29		Narrative attached	RPT.
	30		Battalion resting in DOMINION CAMP. G.23.b.9.6.	RPT.

J.P.B. Wyndham Lieut. Col.
Commdg. 6/West Regt
30-9-18

Narrative of Operations, 6th Battn. Wiltshire Regt. at
ST. ELOI, 29.9.18.

At 2.30 a.m. 28th September, the Battalion assembled in Old FRENCH TRENCH VOORMEZEELE Area disposed as follows for attack on German positions at ST. ELOI.

FRONT LINE. "A" Coy. on left with 20th Bn. Middlesex Regt. on their left.
"C" Coy. on right with 14th Bn. A.& S.H. on right.
Along the line of the OLD FRENCH TRENCH. O2.a.40.60. to O.32.d.00.85.
"B" Coy. in support
"D" Coy. in Reserve in VOORMEZEELE SWITCH TRENCH from road at O.31.d.30.30. to O.31.d.80.90.
Battalion Headquarters at O.1.b.1.5.

BARRAGE. At 2.30 a.m. a heavy barrage was opened along the front of the BELGIAN ARMY. At 5.25 a.m. Barrage opened on the Battalion front, and the Battalion moved forward to the attack reaching their first objective at 6.20 a.m. where a pause was made while the ground in front of and at final objective was searched by the barrage while Infantry were consolidating.
At 7.21 a.m. the advance was resumed and the Battalion reached their final objective the line O.2.d.45.00. MIKHOF FARM.
During the whole of these operations the battalion was under Artillery and Heavy Machine Gun Fire and had numerous strong points to assault which they carried with determination killing and capturing 200 of the enemy, 2 guns, 15 machine guns, and 4 trench mortars and losing 1 Officer 7 Other Ranks killed and 45 Other Ranks wounded and missing.
This line was held till the evening of 29th September when the Battalion was withdrawn on 34th Division taking up positions along DAMSTRASSE.

CONFIDENTIAL No 242

WAR DIARY
6th Batt Wiltshire Regt.
Oct 1 - 31st 1918

Volume AO.

WAR DIARY
or
INTELLIGENCE SUMMARY.
(Erase heading not required.)

Army Form C. 2118.

Place	Date	Hour	Summary of Events and Information	Remarks and references to Appendices
	1		Battalion resting in DOMINION CAMP. Transport at SCOTTISH CAMP. Details and Billets personnel at ABEELE.	N.T.
	2		Orders received ca 03.30 to move to WYTSCHAETE by march route. Battalion & Transport moved off at 12.00. arriving at destination 14.00. Strength 24 Officers 504 O.R's.	R.T.3
	3		Orders received at 09.00 to proceed by march route to NEUVE EGLISE. Battalion moved off at 10.00 arriving at camp near SALVATION CORNER at 14.30. Orders received 16.00 to proceed to HELLFIRE CORNER. Battn. entrained at PADDINGTON JUNCTION at 14.30 detraining at HELLFIRE JUNCTION at 01.30. 4th Transport by road to VLAMERTINGHE	R.77.
	4		Battalion moved from station to POTIZZE at 09.00. Billetted in huts & dugouts by 09.30.	R.T.?
	5		Battalion turned out to work on MENIN-YPRES ROAD. Working hours 04.00 to 14.30.	R.T.?
	6		Battalion turned out to work on MENIN-YPRES ROAD. Working hours 04.00 to 14.30.	R.T.?
	7		Battalion turned out to work on MENIN-YPRES ROAD. Working hours 04.00 to 14.30. Camp moved to ZONNEBEKE AREA. Working Parties on YPRES ZONNEBEKE RD. Details by march route. Camp made by dugouts with wire superstr.	R.77.
	8		Battalion working on ZONNEBEKE ROAD. 08.30 to 15.00.	R.77
	9		Battalion working on ZONNEBEKE ROAD. 08.30 to 15.00.	R.77

Army Form C. 2118.

WAR DIARY
or
INTELLIGENCE SUMMARY.
(Erase heading not required.)

Place	Date	Hour	Summary of Events and Information	Remarks and references to Appendices
	10		Battalion working on ZONNEBEKE ROAD. 08.30 to 15.00.	APP1
	11		Battalion working on ZONNEBEKE ROAD. 08.30 to 15.00.	APP1
	12		Working parties on ZONNEBEKE ROAD. Orders received at 21.00.15 move to WULVERGHEM AREA.	APP2
	13		Battalion moved to HELLFIRE JUNCTION entraining at 08.15 detraining PADDINGTON JUNCTION 12.30 and settled in CAMP (T.4.a. 10.0 Sheet 28) 14.30. Junks & Dugouts. Transport by road from VLAMERTINGHE arriving 14.30. 15 O.Rs. per A.P.M. 14 Div. as stragglers Post. 10. O.Rs. per A.P.M. 14 Div. as prisoners escort. Lieut. J.A. Gallery joined for duty.	APP2
	14		Inspection & refitting of troops. Warning Order received to be ready to move at 2 hour notice.	APP4
	15		Orders received 01.30 to move to MESSINES Area. Battalion & Transport moved off by march route via NEUVE EGLISE to road S. of MESSINES at 08.00. arriving 11.30. Battalion entrained & took over support from YORK. & LANCS. Regt. arriving in camp 23.00. Transport by road to TEA CAMP near WULVERCHEM. Headquarters located at German Pill Box in Ruin at P.31.d.2.4. Sheet 28.	APP5
	16		Battalion in support to Brigade.	APP5
	17		Lieut. Col. C.O.E. Napier D.S.O. admitted hospital. Major L. Wallace assumes command of Battalion.	APP5

Army Form C. 2118.

WAR DIARY
or
INTELLIGENCE SUMMARY.
(Erase heading not required.)

Instructions regarding War Diaries and Intelligence Summaries are contained in F.S. Regs, Part II. and the Staff Manual respectively. Title pages will be prepared in manuscript.

Place	Date	Hour	Summary of Events and Information	Remarks and references to Appendices
	17.		Battalion in support to Brigade. Warning order received to be prepared to move at short notice. Orders received at 11.50 to move to Houvard Area by Hazel Route. Battalion moved off at 13.30 with 1st line transport (one third remaining under orders of Rly. T.O.) via COMINES to LINSELLES.	app
	18.		Orders received at 04.00 to proceed by Hazel Route to NEUVILLE en FERRAIN. Battalion moved off 13.00, arriving 14.00. Batt. H.Q. W15. a. 8.0, which the Germans had evacuated the previous day. Town full of civilians who were much pleased, gave English troops and gave them a good reception.	app.
	19.		Orders received at 02.00 to move to MONTLEUX by marchroute. Battn. with 1st line transport moved off at 08.30 arriving at MONTLEUX 11.00. Orders received at 14.30 to move to LUINGNE. Battn. moved off at 16.00 arriving in billets 17.08.	app
	20.	11.00	Church Parade. Details from transport rejoined. 3 I.O.R. 1 Section of Y.R.B. attached to battalion.	app
	21.		2nd line transport rejoined Battalion. Inspection of clothing + equipping. Lieut. L. Wing joined for duty. Orders received 14.00 notifying that Bde. relief in front line by 16th Manchesters 8.14 A.T.S.M.	app
	22.		Orders received for Battn. to relieve 16th Manchester Bgt. in Divs. line by Battn. arrangements. C.O., Adjt. + Coy. Commanders reconnoitred front line + arranged relief. 'D' Coy. (Right) front near WAREOING. 'B' Coy. (Left) front ESPIERRES.	app.

WAR DIARY
or
INTELLIGENCE SUMMARY.
(Erase heading not required.)

Army Form C. 2118.

Place	Date	Hour	Summary of Events and Information	Remarks and references to Appendices
	23.		Battn. marched off at 16.00 to front line. Relief completed by 23.30. Battn. H.Q. at CLERQUANT FARM. Sheet 34. Transport moved to CROMBION area. Strength 26 Officers. 559 O.Rs.	R.77.
	24		1 Officer 2 O.R. detailed on covering party to R.E. Bridging Canal at L'ESCAUT. 2 Lieut. Jones wounded, at duty, 4 O.Rs wounded.	R.77.
	25		Patrolling on River L'ESCAULT front. Wounded work 3. Officer 1/6th R.E. & Davies. 1 Officer wounded. 1 Lieut. Y. Wing took over command of "D" Coy.	R.77.
	26		2nd Lieut. Nixon killed. 2 O.R. wounded. Support Coys A" & "C" relieved. Front line Coys. Relief completed 20.30. Warning Order received 21.00 that Battn. will be relieved night of 27/28 Oct.	R.77.
	27		Orders received at 13.30 that Battn. will be relieved on left front by 16th Manchesters. Right front by Battn. of 121 Bde. 40 Div. Arrangements to be made by Battn. concerned. Battn. to move on relief to billets vacated by 16th Manchrs 1917 at DOTTIGNIES. Relief of Left Coys. complete by 22.00. Right front Coy. by 03.30.28th. Battn. in new billets by 04.00. Platoons moving off as they were relieved. 2 O.R Wounded.	R.77.
	28		Resting of Battn. Refitting. Winter clothing issued.	R.77.
	29		Training under Coy. arrangement. 1 O.R. accidentally wounded died at C.C.S.	R.77.
	30		Training under Coy. arrangement. Court of Enquiry on death of No. 19 Pte. Elvins. Orders received at 20.00 that Battn. will move to LUINGNE AREA. Take over billets of 29th D.L.I. on 31st.	R.77.
	31.		Battn. marched off at 13.30, arriving in new area at 15.30. Headquarters located at S.23.d.20.90. Sheet 29. Transport moved from CROMBION to a position in new area greater than 6 miles from Battn. for Blankets & Blanket retasking Relieving 29th D.L.I.	R.77.

COMMANDING 6th Battn. Wiltshire Regiment

6th Batt. WILTSHIRE REGT.

WAR DIARY

1 – 30 November 1918

Volume 40.

96 4 3

Confidential

Army Form C. 2118.

WAR DIARY
or
INTELLIGENCE SUMMARY.
(Erase heading not required.)

Place	Date	Hour	Summary of Events and Information	Remarks and references to Appendices
Field	November 1918.			
	1		Battalion in Billets at LUINGNE. Headquarters "B" & "C" Companies Bathing and disinfecting clothing with Foden disinfector at HERSEAUX. Church parade at 16.00 hours. Strength of Battn. 46 Officers 463 O.Rs. No. 204631 Sgt. England A.P. "A" Coy. & No. 208888 Pte. Brent "C" Coy. awarded Military Medal. Authority: 14th Division Routine Order 68/188 dated 31.10.18.	appx
	2		Training under Coy. arrangements. Warning Order received at 11.00 hours that Battn. will move to WATTRELOS on 3.11.18. Orders received at 20.00 to proceed by march route on 3.11.18. Lieut. E.D. Taylor admitted to Hospital.	appx
	3		Battalion marched to WATTRELOS via HERSEAUX parading 09.00 hours arriving new area 11.45. Headquarters located at A.22.a.8.4. Sheet 34. 34 Officers 524 O.Rs. 1 O.R. joined from D.I.B.D.	appx
	4		Battalion parade 09.00. Training under Company arrangements.	
	5		Battalion parade 09.00 training under Company arrangements.	appx
	6		Battalion (less "A" Coy) paraded for training 09.00. "A" Coy. field firing on range at G.3.6.4.0. Sheet 34. Bomb Mortar on No. 20904H. Sgl. Sec. held at H.Q. Hidebarath gl. at A.12.d.4.4. Sheet 34.	appx

WAR DIARY
or
INTELLIGENCE SUMMARY.
(Erase heading not required.)

Army Form C. 2118.

Place	Date	Hour	Summary of Events and Information	Remarks and references to Appendices
	November 1918			
Field	6th		Warning Order received 22.30 that Battn. will move to new area in support on 8th inst. Location 34.B.4.0. 40.45.	APX
	7		Training under Company arrangements. Specialists under Specialist Officers. Orders received 21.30 that Brigade will move to area to be vacated by 43rd Bde. on 8.11.18 by march route.	APX
	8		Battalion marched 13.230 & marched to QUEVAUCAMP Bu.C.2.3 via PETIT Sheet 37 AUDENARDE arriving in billets at 16.15. Capt. L.E. Daniels proceeded to 14 Div. Reception Camp for duty.	APX
	9		Orders received 09.30 to move to COYGHEM. Battn. moved at 11.00, arrived in new area 12.35. Headquarters at U.19.c.2.2. Transport U.25.a.30.80. Sheet 29. Major L. Wallace & Capt. C.L.H. Jenkyn authorised to wear badges of rank of Lt.Col. & Major respectively. Authority 14 Div. A5/106 - 9.11.18. Orders received at 23.35 to move to DOTTIGNIES on 10.11.18.	APX
	10		Battalion marched off 11.00 arriving in billets at DOTTIGNIES 12.00. Headquarters at B.5.c.8.4. Sheet 34. Transport at T.23.a.2.2. Sheet 29. 1 O.R. rejoined from Hospital.	APX

Army Form C. 2118.

WAR DIARY
of
INTELLIGENCE SUMMARY.
(Erase heading not required.)

Instructions regarding War Diaries and Intelligence Summaries are contained in F.S. Regs., Part II. and the Staff Manual respectively. Title pages will be prepared in manuscript.

Place	Date	Hour	Summary of Events and Information	Remarks and references to Appendices
	November 1918			
Lillo	11.		Training under Company arrangement	
			Wire received from 42nd Inf. Bde. that Hostilities cease 11.00 Nov 11th. recd. at 10.30.	1877.
			Church Parade in theatre at 14.30.	
	12.		Battalion Ceremonial Parade at 09.00 to 10.00. Training under Coy. arrangement 10.00 to 12.00.	877.
			Wire received from G.O.C. 14th Division.	
			Congratulatory letter received from G.O.C. 14th Division.	
	13.		Battalion Ceremonial parade 09.00. Training under Coy arrangement 10.00 to 12.00.	877.
			& inspection of Battn. by Medical Officer.	
			No. 44731 Pte. Reynolds tried by F.G.C.M. Lieut. E.J. Deacon rejoined from	
			Hospital and relinquishes the Acting rank of Capt.	
			Orders received at 18.00 to move to HERSEAUX area on 14th	
	14.		Battalion marched off 10.00 via QUEVAUCAMP & PETIT AUDENARDE	877.
			arriving at Billets in WATTRELOS (Sheet 34.A.22.a.5.6) at 12.15.	
			Transport at A.22.a.2.5. Sheet 34.	
			2nd Lieut. R.D. Loy awarded Military Cross. Authority:- 14th Div. Routine Order 14/207. 13.11.18	
	15		Battn. Ceremonial Parade 09.00. Training under Coy. arrangement 10.00 to 12.00.	877.
			Proceedings of F.G.C.M. on No. 44731. Pte. Reynolds promulgated.	

Army Form C. 2118.

WAR DIARY
or
INTELLIGENCE SUMMARY.
(Erase heading not required.)

Instructions regarding War Diaries and Intelligence Summaries are contained in F. S. Regs. Part II. and the Staff Manual respectively. Title pages will be prepared in manuscript.

Place	Date	Hour	Summary of Events and Information	Remarks and references to Appendices
Field	November 1918			
	16.		Battalion ceremonial parade 09.00 to 10.00. Training under Coy. arrangements 10.00 to 12.00. Capt. L.B. Martin proceeded to HARDELOT PLAGE Rest Camp. 2nd Lieut. F.J. Smith joined from D.I.B.D. for duty. 2nd Lieut. H. McCormick evacuated to U.K. sick on 3.11.18. State of strength – see H. Appendix.	Appx
	17.		Church Parade in Cinema Hall 10.00. C.E. 11.15 Non-conformist. Thanksgiving Service at CIRQUE TOURCOING. 5 Officers 55 O.R's attended, marching past Lieut. General Sir C.W. Jacobs. K.C.B. Acting 2nd. Army Commander, after service.	Appx
	18.		Ceremonial parade 09.00 to 10.00. Training under Coy. arrangements 10.00 to 12.00. Orders received to form Agricultural Coy. for work on French farms. Battn. to find Coy. Commander, Platoon Officer + 50 O.R's. Inspection of Transport by D.A.D.V.S. 14th Division 12.00. Football + Boxing in the afternoon.	Appx
	19.		Battalion ceremonial parade 09.00 to 10.00. Training under Coy. arrangements 10.00 to 12.00. Football in the afternoon.	Appx
	20.		Battalion ceremonial parade 09.00 to 10.00. Training under Coy. arrangements 10.00 to 12.00. 2nd Lieut. P.J. Nolan appointed the Divisional Agricultural Officer. Lecture on "Work of the Army" at TOURCOING by C. Smart Simpson. 10 Officers + 50 O.R's attended.	Appx

Army Form C. 2118.

WAR DIARY
or
INTELLIGENCE SUMMARY.
(Erase heading not required.)

Place	Date	Hour	Summary of Events and Information	Remarks and references to Appendices
Field	November 1918			
	21.		Battalion marched to HERSEAUX for Brigade Ceremonial Parade & took Bat, parading 08.00, returning to billets 12.00. Football &c. in the afternoon. Lieut. Col. C.J.E. Rapson D.S.O. rejoined from D.I.B.D. & assumed command. Major L. Wallace & Capt. L.H.H. Jenkyn relinquish Acting Ranks of Lieut. Col. & Major. Major L. Wallace takes over 2nd in Command. Capt. Jenkyn resumes Command of "A" Coy.	P247.
	22.		Battalion Ceremonial parade 09.00 to 10.00. Training under Coy. arrangements 10.00 to 12.00. Football & Boxing in the afternoon. Agricultural Coy. so OR under Capt. the Hon. D.K. Watson & 2nd Lieut. St. Plumbley paraded for work at 08.00. 1 OR. joined from Garrison Base Depot. French classes opened.	P247.
	23.		Brigade march past Official Commander Lieut. Gen. Perina at HERSEAUX. Battn. parading 07.30 & returning to Billets 12.30.	P247.
	24.		Church Parade L. of C. 10.00. Non-con. 11.15 at Cinema Hall.	P247.
	25.		Training under Coy. arrangements 09.00 to 12.00. Football &c. in the afternoon.	P247.
	26.		Battalion route march. Paraded 09.00 route via LEERS, LEERS NORD, ESTAMPUIS, WATTRELOS. Battn. reached billets 11.50.	P247.

WAR DIARY
or
INTELLIGENCE SUMMARY.
(Erase heading not required.)

Army Form C. 2118.

Place	Date	Hour	Summary of Events and Information	Remarks and references to Appendices
	November 1918			
Field	27.		Demonstration Platoon training under C.O. at 09.00. Battn. bathed at HERSEAUX.	APP.
			Drums proceeded by lorry to CROIX for practice Searchlight tattoo.	
	28.		Demonstration Platoon training under C.O. at 09.00. Medical Inspection by M.O.	APP.
			Training under Coy. arrangements. Football match v. 14th R.W.S.H. at 14.30.	
			8 Officers & 92 O.R. attended lecture at TOURCOING at 15.00 by Sir F. Younghusband	
	29		Training under Coy. arrangements. Demonstration Platoon under C.O. at 09.00.	APP.
			50 O.R. attended lecture at TOURCOING by Mr. S.B. Taylor on Demobilisation	
			Battn. H.Q. moved to Billet No 58 Rue de Roubaix Sheet 34/A.21.c.8.0.	
			Capt. Barty proceeded to U.K. to attend course at Trinity College, Oxford	
	30.		Battalion parade at 09.30. & marched to HERSEAUX	APP.
			Drill competition judged by B.G.C. 42nd Inf. Bde - won by A.Coy. 13.00	
			Capt. L.H. Bone, Lieut. C.J. Orley, & 2nd Lieut. Morton joined for duty from D.B.D.	
			3 O.R. rejoined from Garrison Base Depot.	
			Lieut. C.D. Taylor transferred to U.K. 19.11.18 & Struck off Strength.	

John Walmsley ?
Commanding 6th Batt. Wiltshire Regt

WR 44

CONFIDENTIAL

War Diary

1st Battn Wiltshire Regiment

From December 1st 1918
To December 31st 1918

Volume 36.

WAR DIARY or INTELLIGENCE SUMMARY

Army Form C. 2118.

Place	Date	Hour	Summary of Events and Information	Remarks and references to Appendices
	DECEMBER 1918		Battalion in billets at WATTRELOS.	
	1.		Capt. J. H. Bone in command R'Boy.	
			Church Parade 10.00 hours in Cinema Hall C. of E. – 11.15 in Cinema. Nonconformist. 1 Officer, 16 O.R. of 1/2nd Y.K.L.B. proceed to HERSEAUX, & cease to be attached to the Battalion for rations from 2nd.	RPF
	2.		Battalion Ceremonial Parade at 09.15 hours. Training under Boy. arrangement. Lieut. Col. C. E. E. Kaye, D.S.O. proceeded to U.K. to report to Senior Officers School of Tactics. Major B. Wallace assumed Command of Battalion. Capt. Payne assumed duties of 2nd. in Command. 1 O.R. to D.I.B.D. & Strike off. Shorthand & Typist Classes commenced.	RPF
	3.		Battalion Ceremonial Parade at 09.15 hours. Training under Boy. arrangement. Torchlight Tattoo, ROUBAIX. Battalion Band took part.	RPF
	4.		Battalion Ceremonial Parade at 09.15 hours. Training under Boy. arrangement. Divisional Boxing Tournament commenced at TOURCOING. Shorthand Y'phonet. Classes.	RPF
	5.		Training under Boy. arrangement. Rifle Inspection. Baths at HERSEAUX. Book-keeping class opened.	RPF
	6.		Battalion Ceremonial Parade at 09.15 hours. Training under Boy. arrangement. L/Sgt. Singland awarded Croix de Guerre. 1,2 & 4 Rifles Cambridge Concert for Cinema. Platoon visited LILLE. Pte. Whitlock reached Final in Bn. Boxing Competition.	RPF
	7.		Inspection by G.O.C. 14th Div. at HERSEAUX. Battalion paraded 08.15 hours. 1 O.R. rejoined from Garrison Base Depot. Lecture by Col. Bourne at Convent Hall. HERSEAUX, on "Settlement of Soldiers on the Land". Battalion Concert at Cinema.	RPF

WAR DIARY
or
INTELLIGENCE SUMMARY.
(Erase heading not required.)

Army Form C. 2118.

Place	Date	Hour	Summary of Events and Information	Remarks and references to Appendices
	DEC 1916			
	9	10-15	Volunteer Parade 10-15. Billet Inspection by C.O., 2nd i/c, & M.O.	R77
			Battalion Ceremonial Parade 09-15. Training under Coy. arrangement. Court of enquiry held on whereabouts of No 18692. Pte. L.W. Wilson. Proceedings & B.115. Despatched to Brigade. 50 O.R. joined from Garrison Base Depot. Capt. C.W.N. Jerhyn arrived 2nd i/c of Bn. & 1 O.R. Base proceeded to 2nd Bn. for duty.	R77
	10		Inspection by Army Commander at 11.00 hours at MOUVEAUX 36/F. 25. a. 3. Battalion paraded Squared at 07.30 hours, & moved to Inspection. Book-keeping class.	R77
	11		Battalion parade 09.00 hours. Inspection of draft by C.O. 4 O.R. "War Worn" to depot, DEVIZES. Shorthand & Signal Classes.	R77 R77
	12		Battalion parade 09.00 hours. Demonstration platoon after Bn. Parade. Book-keeping Class. 1 Miner demobilized.	R77 R77
	13		Lieut. J. Whig. proceeded to 2nd Army H.Q. for special legal duty. Battalion parade 09.00 hours. Demonstration after Battn. Parade. 1 Platoon 'B' Coy proceeded to LILLE for the day. Shorthand & Signal Classes. 3 Miners demobilized. Court of enquiry held on the loss of a revolver in charge of No 41593. Pte Bowns L.Y. 1 O.R. rejoined from Garrison Base depot.	R77 R77 R77
	14		Battalion parade 09.00. Demonstration platoon parade after Battln Parade. Medical Inspection of Men on parade ground. 14 Miners demobilized. 1 Platoon 'C' Coy. proceeded to LILLE for the day.	R77 R77

WAR DIARY
or
INTELLIGENCE SUMMARY.
(Erase heading not required.)

Army Form C. 2118.

Place	Date	Hour	Summary of Events and Information	Remarks and references to Appendices
	DEC. 15.		Church Parade in Cinema Hall 10.15 hours. Inspection of Billets by C.O. at 2nd Yr.	app.
	16.		Battalion Parade 09.00 hours. Training under Coy. arrangements & demonstration Platoon after Batt. Parade.	app.
	17.		Battalion Parade 09.00 hours. 1 Platoon "D" Coy proceeded to LILLE for the day, in buses.	app.
	18.		Battalion Parade 09.00 hours. Training under Company arrangements & Demonstration Platoon after Batt. Parade. 1 Platoon "B" Coy proceeded to LILLE. Miners demobilized. Training under Coy. arrangements. Battalion bathing. "4" Miners demobilized.	app.
	19.		Battalion Parade 09.00 hours. Training under Coy. arrangement. "A" Coy. on rifle range. 1 Platoon "C" Coy. proceeded to LILLE for the day.	app.
	20.		Battalion parade 09.00 hours. Training under Coy. arrangements after Bn. Parade.	app.
	21.		Battalion bathing, & Blankets passed through steam disinfector. Training under Coy. arrangements. 1 Platoon "D" Coy to LILLE for the day.	app.
	22.		Church Parade in Cinema Hall 10.15. Inspection of Billets by C.O. Y 2nd Yr.	app.
	23.		Battalion parade in trees at 09.00 hours. Training under Coy. arrangements after Batt. Parade. Shortened Book Keeping Classes.	app.
	24.		Battalion parade in trees at 09.00 hours. Training under Coy. arrangements after Battn. parade. Court of Enquiry held re absence of 70.48303 Cpl. H. Askew "B" Company. Proceedings forwarded to 121st Infantry Brigade.	app.

WAR DIARY
or
INTELLIGENCE SUMMARY.
(Erase heading not required.)

Army Form C. 2118.

Instructions regarding War Diaries and Intelligence Summaries are contained in F.S. Regs., Part II. and the Staff Manual respectively. Title pages will be prepared in manuscript.

Place	Date	Hour	Summary of Events and Information	Remarks and references to Appendices
	DEC. 25		Church Parade 11.15 in Cinema Hall. Men had Christmas dinner together in factory located at 3½/M.2.7. Hastily improvised as a Dining Room. Concert held in Cinema Hall at 19.00. 1 O.R. joined from J.I.B.D.	APP?
	26.		Training under Coy. arrangements. Battalion Officers' Mens & Corps Xmas dinner.	APP?
	27.		Battalion parade at 09.00 hours. Training under Coy. arrangements after Bn. Parade	APP?
	28.		Battalion Kit Inspection by C.O. Skin inspection by M.O.	APP?
	29.		Church Parade 10.15 in Cinema Hall. Inspection of billets by C.O. & 2nd i/c.	APP?
	30.		Battalion parade 10.00 hours. Shorthand & Book keeping classes. Billets inspected by G.O.C. 14 Division.	APP?
	31.		Battalion parade at 09.00 hours. Training under Coy. arrangements after Bn. Parade. 1 O.R. demobilised.	APP?

[signature]

WO 45

WAR DIARY
6 Bn 14th WILTSHIRE REGT.
Jany 1st 1919
to
Jany 31st 1919
VOLUME A1

CONFIDENTIAL 14/

Army Form C. 2118.

WAR DIARY
or
INTELLIGENCE SUMMARY.
(Erase heading not required.)

Instructions regarding War Diaries and Intelligence Summaries are contained in F.S. Regs., Part II. and the Staff Manual respectively. Title pages will be prepared in manuscript.

Place	Date	Hour	Summary of Events and Information	Remarks and references to Appendices
	1919 January			
	1st		Battalion in Billets at Watreloo. Church parade 10.30 hr. Battalion trained at Herseaux. Lt. Col. G.F. Capron D.S.O. to be Brig. Major. Lt. F.H. Acourt in command of D Company.	n.a.r.
	2nd		Battalion Parade at 09.00 hrs – Route March – Educational classes. Recreational Training. 1 Platoon visited Lille.	n.a.r.
	3rd		Training under Company arrangements – Educational classes – Recreational Training.	n.a.r.
	4th		Kit Inspection by Commanding Officer – Kirn Inspection by reserve officer.	n.a.r.
	5th		Church Parade at 10.15 in Cinema – Inspection of Billets by Commanding Officer and Second-in-command. 2nd Lt. W.J. Ryle appointed Assistant Adjutant. 2 Other ranks demobilized.	n.a.r.
	6th		Battalion Parade in N.C.O.s – Training under Company arrangements. Recreational Training and Educational classes. 1 O.R. demobilized.	n.a.r.

Army Form C. 2118.

WAR DIARY
or
INTELLIGENCE SUMMARY.
(Erase heading not required.)

Place	Date	Hour	Summary of Events and Information	Remarks and references to Appendices
1919	January		Sheet II	
	7th		Battalion parade in mass – Training under Company arrangements – Recreational Training and Educational Classes. 1 Other rank demobilised.	w.o.
	8th		Battalion bathed at Herseaux. 1 Other rank joined from Reinforcement camp.	w.o.
	9th		Battalion Route March – Recreational training and Educational Classes. 1 Platoon visited Lille.	w.o.
	10th		Training under Company arrangements – Inspection of Billets &c by A.D.M.S. 1 Other rank to Rouen for duty in England.	w.o.
	11th		Kit Inspection by Commanding Officer & Second in Command – Medical Inspection by M.O. 80 Other ranks attended Cine Lecture at Herseaux on "Sea Power" by Mr. P. Maddock. 6 Other ranks demobilized.	w.o.
	12th		Church parade in Cinema at 10–15 – Inspection of Billets by C.O. and Second in Command. Educational Classes Parade for each morning.	w.o.

WAR DIARY
INTELLIGENCE SUMMARY
(Erase heading not required.)

Army Form C. 2118.

Place: Sheet III

Date	Hour	Summary of Events and Information	Remarks and references to Appendices
1919 January			
13th		Battalion Parade at 09.15 - Lecture by Capt. Benham-Carter. 1 Platoon to field. No 148/80 Cpl W Dudley awarded Belgian Croix de Guerre. Capt. J. E. Welsh proceeded to 4th F.A. for duty. 7 O.R. demob'd.	nil
14th		Battalion Parade at 09.15 - Training under Company arrangements. Educational Classes of Educational Training. Court of Enquiry held in loss of 3 Bicycles, proceedings forwarded to HQ 4th Infantry Brigade.	nil
15th		Baths at Hervanne. Training under Company arrangements. Educational Classes. Educational Training.	nil
16th		Battalion Parade at 09.15 - Training under Company arrangements. Educational Classes. Educational Training.	nil
17th		Inspection by Brigadier Gen. Dobbin. 1 Company marching order. 1 Company Battle order. 1 Company's Belts inspected, and 1 Company Kit Inspection.	nil
18th		Training under Company arrangements. Educational Training. Educational Classes and 1 Platoon visited Lille.	nil

WAR DIARY or INTELLIGENCE SUMMARY

Army Form C. 2118.

Place: Sheet IV

Date	Hour	Summary of Events and Information	Remarks and references to Appendices
1919 January 19th		Church Parade 10-15 in Cinema Hall. Inspection of Billets by Commanding Officer and Second in Command. Col. G.F.O. Thorn D.S.O. resumed Command of Battalion. Major Wallace assumed 2nd in Command. Capt. Cash Entryman assumed Command of A Company. 222 other ranks demobilized.	not
20th		Battalion Parade 09-15. – Training under Company arrangements. Educational Classes. Recreative Training. 227. A. Barton demobilized + 35 O.R. 1 O.R. killed by French Civilian.	not
21st		Lecture at Concert Hall. Research on "Round the World in War time" by E. Kingston - 60 other ranks attended. Battalion Parade at 09-30. – Educational Classes. Recreative Training. Lt. J. Soley demobilized + 32 other ranks.	not
22nd		Bath at Herseaux. Educational Classes. Recreative Training. 1 Party demobilized + 27 other ranks. Court Martial on 6118 Acken for "Absence without leave".	not
23rd		Training under Company arrangements – Educational Classes + Recreative Training.	not

WAR DIARY
INTELLIGENCE SUMMARY.
(Erase heading not required.)

Army Form C. 2118.

SHEET V

Place	Date	Hour	Summary of Events and Information	Remarks and references to Appendices
1919 January	24th		Battalion Route March - Inspection of Boots by Bn. Sergt. A.O.D. C.S.M. Elliven summer MSM - Educational Classes & Recreational Training	W.R.
	25th		Kit Inspection by C.O. - Education Classes & Recreational Training. 16 O.R. demobilised	W.R.
	26th		Church Parade 10.15 - Guard 1 NCO + 4 men detailed for Belgian Border Front Hévenne	W.R.
	27th		Roll Kit day. Pte Wilson, Wykeham and 32 other rks. & horses sent to Louvelle to demobilise. Training under Company arrangements - Educational Classes and Recreational Training. J.L. & Wiggins & 19 O.R. demobilised	W.R.
	28th		Training under Company arrangements - Educational Classes & Recreational Training. 16 O.R. demobilised	W.R.
	29th		Battalion Bathed at Hévenne - Educational Classes & Recreational Training. L/Sgt Roberts + 27 O.R. demobilised	W.R.

Sheet VI

1919 January

30: Training under Company arrangements.
Agricultural Company schedules and officers and
other ranks returned to units.
Educational classes recommenced training.

WKR

31: Battalion parade on Battle Order at 09.30 hrs.
Educational classes recommenced training.
Inspection of Billets by A.D.M.S.
Terms of Enquiry held on Pte Boley, proceeding to
forward to Brigade.
Interrogation of Court Martial Proceedings on Lieut. Col. Boyle
held at Tournay on 26/1/19 by Brigadier General H.T Dobbin D.S.O.

WKR

CONFIDENTIAL

6th Battalion, Wiltshire Regt. Vol "46"

WAR DIARY

1st – 28th February 1918.

VOL 42

Army Form C. 2118.

WAR DIARY
or
INTELLIGENCE SUMMARY. 6th Battalion Wiltshire Regt.
(Erase heading not required.)

Instructions regarding War Diaries and Intelligence Summaries are contained in F. S. Regs. Part II. and the Staff Manual respectively. Title pages will be prepared in manuscript.

Place	Date	Hour	Summary of Events and Information	Remarks and references to Appendices
	February			
Waterloo	1-2-19		Battalion in Billets at Waterloo – Strength 506 O.R. Two Inspections by Commanding Officer. One Officer & 23 Other ranks proceeded for demobilization. Educational classes & Recreational Training.	A/C
	2-2-19		Church Parade at 10-15 hrs. Inspection of Billets by Commanding Officer. 1 Officer & 10 Other ranks proceeded for demobilization.	A/C
	3-2-19		Battalion Parade in Mass at 09-30 hrs. Training under Company arrangements after Batta Parade. Educational Classes. Recreational Training. 1 Officer & 13 Other ranks demobilised.	A/C
	4-2-19		Training under Company arrangement. Educational Classes. Recreational Training.	A/C
	5-2-19		Battalion Routine as previous. Educational Classes. Recreational Training.	A/C

WAR DIARY
or
INTELLIGENCE SUMMARY.
(Erase heading not required.)

Army Form C. 2118.

Sheet 2.

Place	Date	Hour	Summary of Events and Information	Remarks and references to Appendices
	6-2-19		Battalion Parade at 09.30 hrs. Training under Company arrangements. Educational classes & Recreational Training. 50 Other ranks attended Lecture on "Strategical Geography" by Mr Horace Bellett at Cirque Theatre Roubaix at 16.00 hrs. 1 Officer & 31 O.R. demobilized	pxz
	7-2-19		Training under Company arrangements. Classes & Educational Training & Inspection of Billets by A.D.M.S. 4th Division. 50 O.R. attended Lecture on "The routes from German Dominions to the East Indies" at the Cirque Theatre Roubaix at 16.00 hrs. 31 O.R. demobilized	pxz
	8-2-19		Battalion Kits & Billets inspected by C.O. Educational classes & Recreational Training. 6 O.R. demobilized	pxz
	9-2-19		Church Parade at Trenian Hall 10-15 hrs. 4 O.R. rejoined from 42nd T.M.B. 31 O.R. demobilized	pxz

WAR DIARY
or
INTELLIGENCE SUMMARY.
(Erase heading not required.)

Army Form C. 2118.

Instructions regarding War Diaries and Intelligence Summaries are contained in F. S. Regs., Part II. and the Staff Manual respectively. Title pages will be prepared in manuscript.

Place	Date	Hour	Summary of Events and Information	Remarks and references to Appendices
Sheet 3.				
	10-2-19		Training under Company arrangements Educational Classes Recreational Training 11 OR demobilised.	RTT
	11-2-19		Company & Platoon Training Recreational Training Capt O.B. Tuck rejoined from 239th Div. Employment Coy and resumed Command of C. Company.	RTT
	12-2-19		Battalion baths & Lectures Recreational Training	RTT
	13-2-19		Company & Platoon Training 19 OR demobilised	RTT
	14-2-19		Company & Platoon Training Battalion Lecture on "Re-construction" by Sgt Mack "A" Coy Recreational Training 13 OR demobilised Inspection of Billets by ADMS. 14th Divn.	RTT

WAR DIARY
or
INTELLIGENCE SUMMARY.
(Erase heading not required.)

Army Form C. 2118.

Instructions regarding War Diaries and Intelligence Summaries are contained in F. S. Regs., Part II. and the Staff Manual respectively. Title pages will be prepared in manuscript.

Place	Date	Hour	Summary of Events and Information	Remarks and references to Appendices
Sheet 4.				
	15-2-19		Battalion Kits inspected by Commanding Officer. Recreational Training. 9 O.R. demobilised.	R77
	16-2-19		Church Parade at 10.15 a.m. 3 O.R. demobilised.	R77
	17-2-19		Training under Company arrangements. Recreational Training. 5 O.R. demobilised.	R77
	18-2-19		Training under Company arrangements. Recreational Training.	R77
	19-2-19		Battalion paraded at Baths Hesdin for change of under clothing. Recreational Training.	R77
	20-2-19		Company Platoon Training. Recreational Training. 2 O.R. demobilised.	R77
	21-2-19		Training under Company arrangements. Inspection of Billets by A.D.M.S. 4th Div. Recreational Training.	R77

Army Form C. 2118.

WAR DIARY
or
INTELLIGENCE SUMMARY.
(Erase heading not required.)

Instructions regarding War Diaries and Intelligence Summaries are contained in F. S. Regs., Part II. and the Staff Manual respectively. Title pages will be prepared in manuscript.

Place	Date	Hour	Summary of Events and Information	Remarks and references to Appendices
Sheet 5	22-2-19		Battalion Bathed at Moreuvre Recreational Training	R77
	23-2-19		Church Parade at the Mole Cine de Moulin at 10.15 hrs Billets inspected by Commanding Officer	R77
	24-2-19		Company & Platoon Training Recreational Training	R77
	25-2-19		Training under Company arrangements Recreational Training	R77
	27-2-19		Battalion Bathed at Moreuvre Recreational Training	R77
	28-2-19		Training under Company arrangements. ADMS inspected Billets Recreational Training Battalion Strength Off. 28, OR. 289	R77

6/8 Rifkson Lif/Col
6/ Wilts Regt

WAR DIARY or INTELLIGENCE SUMMARY

Army Form C. 2118.

WILTSHIRE REGT.

Place	Date	Hour	Summary of Events and Information	Remarks and references to Appendices
	1.3.19		Battalion in Billets at Watsulo. Training under Company arrangements.	R77
	2.3.19		Church parade in Cinema Hall Watsulo at 10.15. 2 OR's employed at demobilisation Camp struck off strength. 2 n.c.o.'s & 8 BRs LBW pending repatriation with or without on draft in U.K. + struck off strength.	R77
	3.3.19		Training under Company arrangements. 13 OR's proceeded to concentration Camp for demobilisation. 3 OR employed at demobilisation Camp struck off strength. Lt Morgan proceeded to DAQMG Boulogne for duty & struck off strength.	R77
	4.3.19		Training under Company arrangements. 2 ORs proceeded to concentration Camp for demobilisation.	R77
	5.3.19		Training under Company arrangements. 1 OR rejoined from hospital & taken on strength.	R77
	6.3.19		Battalion bathed at Herseaux. 2 ORs demobilise in U.K. + struck off strength.	R77
	7.3.19		Training under Company arrangements. Battalion billets inspected by ADMS.	R77
	8.3.19		Inspection by C.O. of draft to 2nd Bn of 6th Bucks of 61st Battalion stores dumped at Watsulo ready Guard.	R77
	9.3.19		Church parade in Cinema Hall Watsulo at 10.30 hrs. 114 ORs proceed to Naples for transfer to H.Q. of O'c troops T.S. Car Nicobar & Mt Gallipolieampo as conducting Officers & remain for duty.	R77

WAR DIARY
or
INTELLIGENCE SUMMARY.
(Erase heading not required.)

Army Form C. 2118.

Place	Date	Hour	Summary of Events and Information	Remarks and references to Appendices
	10.3.19		All personnel of C & D Coys moved to A Coy billets at 10.00 hours. Billets vacated were cleared & all government property handed over to the Area Commandant. 10R to Concentration Camp for demobilisation. 10R to UK sick.	app
	11.3.19		Battalion parades at 11.00 hours in full marching order. An attended 2 Pls at Bag Staples struck off Strength. 10R to 7½ Pls Ox & Bucks L.I.	app
	12.3.19		Training in all Company arrangements.	app
	13.3.19		Battalion bathed at Athenée. 10R to Concentration Camp for demobilisation.	app
	14.3.19		The A.D.M.S. inspected billets at 15.00 hours.	app
	15.3.19		The L.O. inspected billets & kits at 11.00 hours.	app
	16.3.19		Church Parade held in Cinema Hall, Wattrelos at 10.00 hours.	app
	17.3.19		Training in all Company arrangements. 2/Lt Nolan crossed Hygiene Board by W.O. & struck off Strength.	app
	18.3.19		Armourer Inspector inspected Lewis Guns at Tourcoing at 10.00 hours & Rifles at Wattrelos at 22.30 hours. 10R to 7½ Pls Ox & Bucks L.I. & struck off Strength.	app
	19.3.19		Training in all Company arrangements. 2/Lt Plumbly to Concentration Camp for demobilisation.	app
	20.3.19		Training in all Company arrangements.	app
	21.3.19		Training in all Company arrangements. 10R proceeded to 7½ Pls Ox & Bucks L.I. & struck off Strength.	app

WAR DIARY
or
INTELLIGENCE SUMMARY.
(Erase heading not required.)

Army Form C. 2118.

Instructions regarding War Diaries and Intelligence Summaries are contained in F. S. Regs., Part II. and the Staff Manual respectively. Title pages will be prepared in manuscript.

Place	Date	Hour	Summary of Events and Information	Remarks and references to Appendices
	22.3.19		H. Reason to Concentration Camp for demobilisation. Training under Company arrangements.	
	23.3.19		Church Parade in Cinema Hall, Wattles at 10.00 hrs. Inspection of kits by C.O.	
	24.3.19		Capt. V.R.A. Jones M.C. Chaplain proceeds to Etaples for duty & struck off.	
	25.3.19		Training under Company arrangements.	
	26.3.19		Major Wallace proceeded to Courtrai to Headquarters 16th Manchester Regt at 14.00 hours.	
	27.3.19		Battalion bathes at Pierceance. 1 O.R. joined from G.B.D.	
	28.3.19		1 O.R. to Concentration Camp for demobilisation. 9 O.Rs to Concentration Camp for re-engagement furlough. Inspector of kittles by A.D.M.S. at 15.00 hours. Training under Company arrangements.	
	29.3.19		Voluntary Church Parade held in Church Army Hut at 11.15 hours.	
	30.3.19		37 O.Rs to Concentration Camp for re-engagement furlough. 1 O.R. demobilises whilst on leave to U.K. & struck off strength.	
	31.3.19		8 O.Rs to Hospital & struck of strength. 1 O.R. to Concentration Camp for demobilisation & struck off strength. Battalion reduced to Cadre Strength.	

Sr. B. Simpson Lt/Col
Comdg 6/4 Scots
2/IV/19

WAR DIARY
or
INTELLIGENCE SUMMARY.
(Erase heading not required.)

Army Form C. 2118.

6 Wilts Regt

Place	Date 1919 April	Hour	Summary of Events and Information	Remarks and references to Appendices
Wattielo	1		Battalion relieved to Ledeo in Billets Wattielo awaiting instructions. Officer Strength 17 OR Strength 62.	APP.
	2		do do	APP.
	3		1 O.R. to 74 Div + Brooks L9 awaiting instructions	APP.
	4-9			
	10		2 O.R. to 74 Div + Brooks L9	APP.
	11		Cpl Weatherlake 204632 awarded Belgian Decoration Militaire	APP.
	12-13		Awaiting Instructions	APP.
	14		1 O.R. to Concert Camp No 1 for demobilisation	APP.
	15		2 Lt Poole moved here from Wattielo on leave to U.K. return 17.	APP.
	16-21		Awaiting Instructions	APP.
	22		1 Officer + 3 O.R. on trip by lorry to Istand + Bruges —	APP.
	23-27		Awaiting instructions	APP.
	28		Audit Board inspected Regimental accounts.	APP.
	29		Awaiting instructions	APP.
	30		Unit Hqs. Inspected by Maj Gen Torrier Gower and conducted by 14 Divisional Chaplain	APP.

J.F.B. Mayhew Lt Col
Comdg 6/ Wilts R
2.5.19

Confidential

WAR DIARY WO 49

6th Bn Wiltshire Regt

From May 1st 1919
to May 31 1919.

Volume 36.

Army Form C. 2118.

WAR DIARY
or
INTELLIGENCE SUMMARY.
(Erase heading not required.)

Instructions regarding War Diaries and Intelligence Summaries are contained in F. S. Regs., Part II. and the Staff Manual respectively. Title pages will be prepared in manuscript.

Place	Date	Hour	Summary of Events and Information	Remarks and references to Appendices
Watteloo France May	1	9	Cadre in Billets at Watteloo. Awaiting instructions. Strength 10 Officers & its O.R.	R.277.
	2		17 O.R. rejoined from Training H.Q. & Staging Camp	R.277.
	3		Awaiting instructions	R.277.
			2. O.R. taken on strength of its Btn. and 1 Btn. Cadre & Staff Off.	R.277.
	4		1 O.R. rejoined from Training H.Q. & Staging Camp	R.277.
	5		Awaiting instructions	R.277.
	6		16. O.R. proceeded to 2/4th Ox & Bucks L.I. for Transfer	R.277.
	7		2. O.R. rejoined from Training H.Q. & Staging Camp.	R.277.
	8		Awaiting instructions	R.277.
	9		5. O.R. proceeded to 2/4th Ox & Bucks L.I. for Transfer. 9.O.R. proceeded for Leave.	R.277.
	10/11		Awaiting instructions	R.277.
	12		Major Gallwey Capt Luck, Lt Brown, Lt Lovett, 2 Lts Mabey, Coppell, Arthur, Say & Nichts proceeded to Pot W Corps for duty & struck off strength	
	13 + 14		Awaiting instructions	R.277.
	15		1. O.R. transferred to 2/4th Ox & Bucks L.I. on proceeding to Berlin as Officers Servant	R.277.
	16		2. O.R. proceeded to 2/4th Ox & Bucks L.I. for Transfer.	R.277.
	17		2. O.R. rejoined from Touring H.C. & Staging Camp & proceeded to 2/4th Ox & Bucks L.I. for Transfer	R.277.

Army Form C. 2118.

WAR DIARY
or
INTELLIGENCE SUMMARY.
(Erase heading not required.)

Place	Date	Hour	Summary of Events and Information	Remarks and references to Appendices
Waterloo	1919 Feb 18th		Awaiting instructions	277
	19th		Lt. F.C. Blanchard proceeded to Conscit H.Q. for instructions	277
	20-31		Awaiting instructions	277

R F Forbes Capt & Adjt
for.
COMMANDING 6th SERVICE Bn. WILTSHIRE REGIMENT.

Confidential

Vol 50
Content

WAR DIARY
1st Batt. Wiltshire Regt
6 Battn

From 1-6-19
to 9-6-19

Volume 36

WAR DIARY
or
INTELLIGENCE SUMMARY.
(Erase heading not required.)

Army Form C. 2118.

Place	Date 1919	Hour	Summary of Events and Information	Remarks and references to Appendices
Waterloo	June 1		Cadre in Billets at Waterloo awaiting instructions - Warning order received at 10.30 that Cadre less Equipment Guard will proceed to U.K. on 6.6.19.	App
	2 to 5		Closing accounts, inventories & preparing kits in reference to Clauses - Equipment Guard of 2 Officers & 13 O.Rs. proceeded to Nivelles on duty	App
	6		with H.Q of 12 Infy Bde. details. L/Cpl Raper A/Sjt Lt. Att/Dawe and 19 O.Rs proceeded to Erquiert: Camp No 1 at 11.15 en route to U.K.	App
	7		2 Officers & 19 O.Rs entrained St ANDRE at 08.15 & detrained Boulogne at 13.30 & marched to Terlinghtun Camp.	App
	8		19 O.Rs further discharged undertaking & were marched to Marlborough Camp.	App
	9		2 Officers 719 O.Rs marched to Docks for Embarkation to U.K. - destination Denges - having Camp at 08.00.	App

J.F. Mapson Lt Colonel
COMMANDING ... SERVICE Bn. WILTSHIRE REGIMENT